Receipt For Lost Words

Receipt For Lost Words

poems

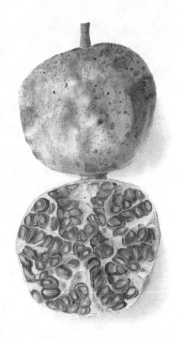

CATHERINE ARNOLD

Bauhan Publishing
PETERBOROUGH NEW HAMPSHIRE
2023

ISBN: 978-087233-372-7
Library of Congress Cataloging-in-Publication Data
Library of Congress Cataloging-in-Publication Data

Names: Arnold, Catherine, 1967- author.
Title: Receipt for lost words : poems / Catherine Arnold.
Description: Peterborough, New Hampshire : Bauhan Publishing, 2023. |
Identifiers: LCCN 2023004637 (print) | LCCN 2023004638 (ebook) | ISBN
    9780872333727 (trade paperback) | ISBN 9780872333734 (ebook)
Subjects: LCGFT: Poetry.
Classification: LCC PS3601.R58266 R43 2023 (print) | LCC PS3601.R58266
    (ebook) | DDC 811/.6--dc23/eng/20230202
LC record available at https://lccn.loc.gov/2023004637
LC ebook record available at https://lccn.loc.gov/2023004638

Book design by Sarah Bauhan; typeset in Arno Pro with Ellington Pro titles.
Cover design by Henry James
Printed by Versa Press
Cover image: Punica granatum: Sweet Green Skinned, 1909 by Elsie E. Lower.
In the public domain. U.S. Department of Agriculture Pomological Watercolor Collec-
tion. Rare and Special Collections, National Agricultural Library, Beltsville, MD 20705

To reach Catherine: www.catherinearnold.com

BAUHAN
PUBLISHING LLC
PO BOX 117 PETERBOROUGH NEW HAMPSHIRE 03458
603-567-4430
WWW.BAUHANPUBLISHING.COM
Follow us on Facebook and Twitter – @bauhanpub

To my two beloveds,
Victor and Stella

CONTENTS

PART ONE

PART TWO: STELLA

PART THREE

PART ONE

The Terms of Silence

The words don't come from the mouth   they come   from the fingers
fingers gripping   the consonants
before she lets them   go.

Kneeling over the book   rocking
syllable by syllable   the words bloom   so that I think   of a rosebush planted
in the ordinary room.

She has memorized them all.

Take the books away   they said   she doesn't understand   the words
The Little House by Virginia Lee Burton
in the brightening   of words   she does not see me   "The little house
shall never be sold for gold or silver . . ."

I watch her again   crouching   in the middle   of the room
all around her   the press and busy thunder
the abducting current   of the world.

"Along came a steam shovel and it dug a road
through the hill . . ."
the words cling   to her fingers   and she shakes them
"Then some trucks with tar and sand . . ."
she is two years old.

For months   after the diagnosis   after the books are hidden
the words persist
walls of perfect text   suspended
trembling slightly   under
the exertions   of her breath.

Sometimes   I thrust my hand in quickly   trying
to touch the words   to watch them stir
"Day followed day, each one a little different from the one before . . ."

Her fingers snap   she does not see me
only the incursion   of the hand
"Year followed year and the apple trees grew old . . ."

And then   the flawless walls   of script   begin to lose
their sharp and   resolution
so that   the pages from one book   are placed inside
the pages from another   then
the pages from all the books   are shuffled
and we fall
from book to book
a little of our certainty   removed
"Now it's not so quiet and peaceful at night
And beneath my scarf is a nose
What a nice little monkey he thought
And a quiet old lady whispering 'hush!'"

The pages are burnished   shine-cut   spliced together
tossing them in   to the lighted center   of the room
stabbing them home
"On the big ship things began to happen . . ."
months pass   still   the books are hidden
the scraps of text   of memory   grow shorter
"After a good meal and a pipe George felt very tired . . ."

She does not use   words   she does not slot them into place
each word is   discovered
each word is found   struck
original and hot
"George had telephoned the fire station!"

I observe   push in the angles   of my sorry head
but I do no more than   dispatch

a few cold thoughts
into the furnace   of the room
"It looked easy. But oh, what happened!
First this—
  and then this!"

Spinning   in the center
conjuring the words   about her
"The man went away. DING A LING A LING!"
the skirt is blazing   airborne.

Months pass and then   there are only single   words
she is three now
and still   she does not see me.

The words begin to disappear   from the day
I hear them at night   they're coming slow   and urgent
"Apple-trees, moon, ship, hush, ding a ling a ling…"
I hear them   on the monitor   "Engine, tired, monkey, scarf…"
she will not speak unless   she is alone
only the direction of the word   remains   fleeing
across the blankets   in the dark.

Months pass.

When occasionally   a word appears   it takes on
the significance   of a lunar eclipse.

And then
there are
no more
words
at all.

Months pass
now she is four.

Everything
is bleeding
away.

After the rosebush
the tenting walls
the fire-skirt
there is nothing.

No words
coming
from the mouth
no words
coming
from the hands.

I am about to learn
the terms
of silence.

* Quoted lines are drawn from: *The Little House* by Virginia Lee
Burton, *Toes, Ears, and Nose!* by Marion Dane Bauer and Karen
Katz, *Goodnight Moon* by Margaret Wise Brown, and *Curious
George* by H. A. Rey.

The Waiting Room

The social worker   cannot arrive   at our names
Mom   Mom   Mom   she calls
mothers in the waiting   chairs
"Mom seems a little upset"
she is referring to all of us   of course
we have grown   conspicuously   similar.

I vowed it wouldn't happen to me   I vowed I would escape it
the closed face   the dull
eyes   the evacuated body
but it's begun   the process   I am slipping.

Each of us   is baffled
each of us knows why   she isn't here.

The body changes   loses its extremities
who needs arms   to wave?   or legs to dance?
we need only
the sort of body
that can wait.

I am watching the officials   cool impervious creatures
reminding me   of the angels in old paintings
beings   who exist   to witness
who come   to close down
the inefficient scenes.

Mom-mom-mom   the angels move the beads across
watching   waiting
combing our hesitations   into their cold hair
if you planted   these creatures   they would not grow
their lean feet   cannot touch the soil.

They stand in   for all officials   for angels and spies
for the triumph   of the resolute   unkind will
for the avoidance   of complication
and there   before them   lands
the mess   of another human soul.

One for the Birds

Before all this began   I used to think   in terms of animals   of
tracking down
I thought in terms   of recognizable warmth
I do not see animals now   I hear them   in the middle of the night
I hear collisions   I hear their breathing
as I wait.

Nature now   is what I see   through glass
the window in the kitchen   the window in her room
I see things that fly
hollow bones
birds through glass   birds scratched in trees.

If you asked me   before I moved in   behind the glass
what is a bird?   I'd have said   they have no mass   no plump
they are not flesh
now   it is through them
I count the hours   of the day
I remind myself   I live on this earth   I have not
despite appearances   settled on another
a blackbird in the morning   a wren in the afternoon
so I advance   bird by bird   toward
the topple of the day.

The term is bird watcher   bird watcher   we say
we do not weigh   or touch them
one for the birds   we say.

Today I spent   hours with Stella   and what did I see?
in the room   we did not move
only the birds moved   outside
outside   they passed away
a bluebird in the morning   a vulture in the afternoon.

Our world grows thinner   lighter
glass is the partition
our world is full   of noise now   roaring
yet because the words   have gone
we've fallen   into silence.

We're separate from the rest now   from the daily human chatter
we're becoming smaller
biting   settling   sleeping
but outside   on the other side   of the glass
the words rise up   the birds fly
I see them pass   tokens of the world before
I learned to notice them
before I became a bird watcher   a word counter
before I knew I'd lose
my memory   and inhabit
this silent   counterclockwise world.

The Walls Will Be Silenced When She Speaks

The house has become a declaration   a legend
and the legend reads   *skirt   trouser   sock*
I cut out the words   and glue them on   considering
their position   how many words will the walls support?
around the words   the space presses
each room I enter now   is composed   of words
advancing
the letters   all in the same font   line up in rows
as neat as tulips
and when it happens   if it happens   if she finds the words
should I peel the tulips from the walls   and make
the house quiet again?
for a moment   I see my daughter
she rustles when she walks
the sound of words   escaping.

Flying Bones

I sing lullabies   I dig holes   in the walls   and sink them in
looking for words   that have no edge
that melt from one blue   to the next
I sing of dolphins and fish   the *ph ph fi fi*
and every word is slow
I let them fall   like a shake of nighttime hair
shaking the syllables out
it makes no difference.

Turn off the lights that would   surround the house
sew shutters   along the outer walls   play music
spinning through   the drowsy air
the tenderness   the faintest brushing of sound against   the eyelids
it makes no difference
I cannot weigh down   the flying bones.

I've tried
all the sacraments
but none of them work   against
the pounding   of the startled heart
sharp legs   pushing
through the paint   of blankets
and each night approaches
trying to balance
expectation   and dread
in the morning   the nights are gathered
bad
awful
worse
Other children sleep
through the night   traitors
I see them floating   doused in milk
mere civilians

and I watch the mothers   after
another night   of voluptuous
uncelebrated
sleep
I study their faces
to see
if the skull   is rising.

An Expedition to Bring Back Coffee

The car stops   the door slides open
I set my fingers on her wrist   for me
it's a question   of covering ground   for her
it's a question   of acquiring weight
the feet must achieve   plausible contact
with the brilliant   speckled   retaliating   ground.

Starbucks   I hold the door open and assess:
body   body   noise between
she steps inside   I steer her toward   the end
of the line   I watch
the arms thrilling
into   the light.

The other bodies are   solidly assembled
each one holding the brocade   the flash and gold
of their smile
grande latte cappuccino   no cinnamon
pound   pound   the feet go down
eyes swivel to appraise   then return quickly   to the straight ahead.

There are those of us who enter   anticipating   difficulty
there are those   who've grown used
to the ease   of domination   and then
there are those   who are oblivious
which comes from
forgotten.
Iced cherry mocha.

That one looked   then placed her eyes   in the lining of her pocket
that one looked   then placed her eyes
devoutly   on the counter
it's our turn now

one small coffee
crucifix slapping   at the throat
that'll be one dollar ninety.
Money handed over   change given   the transaction
completed   but only just begun
in terms of thoughts supplied   thoughts
withheld
as we turn   and move toward the door
eyes watch   from the corner of the room
You need to keep her tethered
he reads his newspaper   his little   stitched-on newspaper
(I am educated   I am solid
I refuse to encounter   the element
of surprise)
and the *New York Times*   is folded
I look back   the *New York Times*   is shaken
I memorize   his unforgiving head.

We are outside now   and my daughter roars
it's the sound of purest red   a shooting pleasure
and while holding   the slightness
of her arm   I look
up to find   the nest   high on the pole
I look up   as I always do   to see if he is there
the osprey
And he is
Not watching   not caring   Yet
as humans do
I pull him down   and make him serve
an intrusion of the fierce   and the beautiful
of the unassimilated will.

Driving through the Cool Low of
the Woman's Heartbeat Voice

Driving through the cool low   of the woman's heartbeat voice
music to rock   your cautious head to sleep
looking back   assessing the angle   of your neck
you remain
in bristling apartness   unsusceptible   it has always been so
hands on the steering wheel   turn the wheel
the book says   they sleep for hours   babies
in my mind   I see them   rows of cradles
nodding   like a line of cresting C's   between
the rules
of a composition book
each one lifting   falling   into the wave of the next
humming into sleep
and then   there are the ones   who can't yield
who aren't drawn   in looping figures
who insist   on the dread   of their listening bones
turn the wheel.

I used to think
you were resolute
not to be moved   not to be whispered
into surrender
I thought defiance   was bold   then
now I know better
your weary eyes   are trying to soften   your lashes combing out
will you sleep
now?
your restlessness is touched again   your spirit rustles up
and you remember.

I check the hands   of the early morning clock   at two   and three   and four
the upstretched neck   the panel of hard feathers
the rest of the world   is settling
while you   are in the act   of being born
legs newly separated   shoulders bared   you've just appeared
time to define yourself
against the dangers   and vertigos
of sleep
time to introduce yourself
to the booming   of the world.
I would spare you   if I could.

The Others

I

The others   I see them going about their   typical
days   surrounded by   the traveling light
their children speak   they dress themselves
they sleep at night   they are typical.

I wonder   as I park the car and watch
my unsuspecting neighbor   why
she is not dancing   it seems a small expression of gratitude
for such exorbitant   good fortune
she stands on the grass   in the yard   this mother
hat rammed down   on pitiless blond hair
outrageously catching   the sun
singing   busy
with this   her unperturbable child
she points to the newspaper   the child picks it up
presents it
I try not   to consider   the implications
of such monstrous alacrity.

Of course   I tell myself   envy is not good.

Nothing happens quickly anymore   the daily effort of lifting
the process of forgetting   and forgiving
I watch my neighbor   with her easy snapping child   I watch the girl pick up
the newspaper   the neighbor laughs   as if   of course   that's what she'd do
I watch the neighbor-mother smiling   showing a little modest pleasure
but she's not astonished   not changed in shape or understanding
and I must stop   for a second
remind myself   to adopt
the right tone   of voice
but as I walk up the drive   I encounter it again

the lack of surprise
on her face
it is the look   of someone accustomed
to the daily arrival   of miracles.

II

I remember the supply   of milk bottles left   on the stone step
the dial displaying the expected number   four pints today   three pints
tomorrow
so their miracles are supplied   and so
they are accepted   without
eagerness
the bottles are taken   placed on the counter
the day is apportioned   and survived.

It wouldn't be like that for me   I would be grateful
and in my mind
I do not wait
for The Milkman   to set the bottles down   I throw myself into the air
I'm no longer somber   or even
human   I've become
what they describe
as pure   animal   spirits.

Each bottle is a word   a sentence   a game
outside my neighbor's house   there are so many   how many sentences
does a typical five-year-old   utter   in a typical day?
a hundred?
a hundred milk bottles   on the stone front step.

I balance a bag of groceries   on my hip   I hold
my daughter's hand

now the neighbor's door has closed
and they carry on
with their reckless   bountiful day.

The milk bottles grow on the step   and I know that inside
the child is still   speaking
and the mother is not   surprised.

Font

It is late   I must print out the words   words
to   paste   over   the   drawers   and   the   fridge
and the cabinet   words to identify   words for my daughter
cup   bowl   spoon   I stare at the words   looking
at the squares   called keys
so I am composing
"Font?" the screen inquires   I see the font   at the entrance to a church
water gathering
water turning into words   streaming over stone
"Font?" the screen demands again   Arial?   Albertus?   Calisto?
Palatino?   Garamond?   All the wonderful   spacious   words
How do I want her to speak?   From which font should I draw?
Times New Roman?
too many vertical lines compelling
discipline and poison
No   I won't choose Roman
Garamond and Palatino?   a couple of characters
from the commedia dell'arte
stripes and the flattery of hungry feet
somersaults turned in late-night straw
a life of promises   and cancellations
tents rolled and packed at midnight
tents struck
and Giles sitting
waiting   hollow with his mouth
open   waiting
for the words   to be provided
he can't afford them   he has no money to place—
and we're back where we started—
no   I won't print the words   for my daughter
in Garamond and Palatino
down the list (shift)
Antique Olive?

too fragile   might spontaneously collapse   I see her crumbling
Omega?   when the last voice shouts
I see the great mouth   opening
into silence
Condensed Clarendon?   I pause
see a London square
dispensing order   from the walls
I pass on   it's too close to Roman   a house
without music   or smoke
even the song   of the bird in the cage   is daunted
down the list again   (shift)
Coronet   Courier   Century Gothic?
there are always
too many choices
when really
there   are   none.

Haircut

I must begin to cut
she must begin to run
I take out the scissors   the clever   wincing blades
the face is poised   the scissors are poised   and I
have a moment to decide
I look into   her private face
the resolution   of her skin
and gauge the quality   of stillness
she jumps   the hair lifts   I had expected that
now she is settled
will the stillness last?

I follow her around the room   the scissors carried
at the level of my mouth   carried like a beak
judging   biting   settling
bring the blades together   *Snap!*
the act supplies   the sound
the sound of pointed   formal work
watch the hair   falling to the floor   it holds together
like thick cloth   it does not flinch or tremble
and I think   of all the times I've tried
to paint hair   lost in the thick of it
trying to pull   the oil sharp   to pull out the strands
to make them crackle.

Here's Dürer's study of a hare
which spells anticipation.
Hare is crouching   watch the light
shuffle across the fur   and think
of the pun   I didn't plan
now   I forget Stella   forget the mother-daughter business
and remember Ireland   a hare running   great gulping bounds
across   an expanse of lighted field   and then

two hares grappling
they did not look like animals.
Joined in terrible compression
were they murdering or mating?

I know now   that nothing reveals
hair   so well   as a single turn of the brush
a stroke of light   emerging from the dark
a single   casual caress.

The Gorgeous Version

This   the voice said (the announcer's voice)
this is the ruby-throated hummingbird   but the bird was colorless   and still
where's the ruby?   I asked   *where's the throat?*
this thing is not humming   it hasn't made a sound
oh   said the voice   *you want the colored version*
and the color entered at the feet   pushing upward
in hot   slippery jolts   pushing
against the bloodless clear   which resisted.

The bird was wet now   it hatched
that's it   I said   with satisfaction
well   of course said the voice   *that's the gorgeous version*
(as if *gorgeous* meant cheap   as if *gorgeous* meant obvious)
I lifted the body and found   the rest of them
their throats straining   their feathers damp
as if they had just   been pulled
from the mutiny   of birth
and of course   what else
would my dreaming mind   hold out   above them
but a word
held
shaking
in the mother's grip
oh yes   I said   *I'll take the gorgeous version.*

Where Does the Fury Come From?

Her rage is cracking slim and hard   against me
I am not seen
she exists   in the dilation   of the pupil
I am crouching
offering pity   and love   as if they are
discrete commodities
cakes upon a plate
offering them   I become absurd
holding the tea set   under my arm.

Where does the fury come from?
A moment ago   the girl I knew—
edges sharp   each line coming to grips—
then a pause   a dimming
the body wavers   falls within
the body has   succumbed.

To be so powerless   not to exist   at all   for her
pouring   the pot   of useless words
it's okay   Stella   it's okay
my body beside hers
fixed   in the rocking-trench
the face rattles   chaos splits the eyes in half.

I make picturesque   gestures
smiting my brow   putting my head   in my hands
such gestures belong   to the stage
but this is where they're found   and taken.

She hits her head against the wall   then
she rushes at the wall   again   plotting
the coordinates   of her position   making her skull
the point   of the pen   *no Stella   no*

I place my hand   between her head   and the wall
how has everything shrunk to this?
the need for the thick of my hand   between the wall   and her skull
how can the terms be so small?

She finds herself   in the mirror
launches herself   down the stream   of the glass
it's okay   Stella   it's okay   holding out   the teapot again
the stacks of quiet china falling
nothing is…
it is all pouring   burning through
and now   she is driving her fingers   into her eyes
I fix   her fingers   with my own
supplying   my presence:
I am here
but she does not want the here—the system
of apologies and haste—she wants
to find   the rending place.

Everything I do   during our waking
hours   is an attempt   to incite
recognition   to touch her fingers   with my own
to bring her eyes   to mine.

There is only the fire   in which we are born—
and it seems to have been going on forever—
and again   she tries to find her body with the wall   her head
touching the points   to the graph
I muffle in   with my restraining   hands
my voice changing   panic-narrow
I am the wick   and she   the flame
and I wonder   if this time
I will be engulfed.

Measuring the Decibels of Silence

When there are no words
we measure the decibels   of silence
with each step   the light is drawn in   drawn back
until she stops   and stands
quite still   no light in her eyes   only
the unkindling   resistance.

She will not eat   she falls asleep again
the bright head   of the needle falling
into the dark case   for sleep is safe   and this sleep
is without illumination.

She is crying   she will not stop   the sound lashes up   batters down
I try to touch her   but the touch of my fingertip   singes the skin
and the pulse of the sound   eradicates
the cool that was left
in the reserve   of the room.

I turn on the music   something we can rely upon
but the room is captured   again   the scream
rises   the music falls
and flickers   barely   on the floor
I go on speaking   I cannot stop myself.

I try to be silent   for I know these words do nothing
she cannot hear them   but the words keep coming
escaping in little rushes
from the unsealed skin
I listen to my voice   listen in surprise   to each protective syllable
and he is speaking too   words overlapping
and still the scream rises
in the center.

We are in the hospital now   she is lying
on the bed   sedated
she is no longer screaming   and we are no longer   speaking.

Give me a sedative   he says   and we sit   paneled to the seats
feeling ancient   feeling unskinned.

The nurse enters   the nurse   whose name is Anne
and she immediately becomes   a legend
because we are unhinged   we are in need
of a redemptive story   we are swinging now   somewhere
high up in the scene   and from here
everything looks sacred
so the nurse walks in…
we sit gripping   the seat   watching Stella sleep
and I think of greyhounds curled
around the feet of women   on medieval tombs
(perhaps it is the hospital precision   we are so cold
there is no vegetation)
and the nurse Anne   brings me a cup of coffee   and brings him
a glass of water   and it seems
to me   an act of legendary   kindness   because
it coincides   with the return of quiet.

A few blocks of silence   placed on the ground
and then the blaze takes hold
and now the silence crackles
we are not present   but suspended   waiting
at the edge of the room   for the next attack.

I am drinking coffee   watching my daughter's face
trying to compel
normality
to enter
and recognize the room.

In Which Doubt Is Introduced

I had a dream last night   what a beginning   don't turn away
and in the dream   I'm looking at a painting   *fresco* fresh
it's fresh in the dream   completely new   though
it's a painting we've seen before
And now you're Botticelli   said the announcer's voice
no room for favor   or passion
I looked at it and saw it new   in the beginning
a painting of   the beginning   *The Birth*
in the center   it wasn't Venus   tucking the serpent tail
of her hair around the long plump   devouring legs   the demure
indirection of the eyes   the air
of extravagant modesty   modesty lush   as a freckled pear
it was a girl   stark   new   a girl
infinitely implausibly familiar   as familiar as the sensation
of my voice catching   in my skin
My girl
her feet were parted slightly   planted on the shell   The Winds were there
as they should have been   but they weren't throwing flowers
they were throwing stones
the words were written on the side
one word to a stone.

I looked at the square feet   set firmly on the shell   at the grooves
cut between the toes   at the precision   every part of her displays
I wondered why
we need words
she is smooth now   she is indestructible
she possesses no clothes   no words   no doubts
she possesses only herself.

She is a fish   a girl   a star
she is original   and fixed.

No one in my waking life   has asked me this
of course   I want my girl to speak   (she is apparently a vessel
in which language can be stored
from which language can be poured)
we talk of receptive language
of expressive language
but what   my dreaming mind inquires
if she is permitted to contain   something else
Herself   only herself
the original   defiant   creature
with her grooved feet   joined in a single fin
speechless and complete
do we have to open her
to coil up the words   and ram them in?

Now she is hungry   thirsty   unapologetic
Now she is perfect.

PART TWO

STELLA

Horse

My feet land on the ground   unsteadily
so that each step unsettles me   even
the central notion   of my spine   forgets itself
before I mount   I am aware of the light
before I mount   I try to take it in   the great warm compass of the animal
sweet fermenting center   it is   against the partial collapsing
staggers of the light   the only forthright thing
the whole dark shape   a solid and
an opening.

Or should I start here?   Mama lifts me high   through the light
higher still   then places me in front
of her   so that   I inhale her with the coil of the animal   together.

I rest against her   the animal against me   pressing my legs
to the breathing hide   the commotion
has receded   the sun lies down   in my warm and necessary flesh
and then   we begin to move   Mama's arms around me   crossing   bracing
I feel my body   and it is whole
I am arrested   blinking   in this new sensation   I let out
a small starting   sound
of recognition
and when the horse moves   forward in the first instant   I find
that I am already   accustomed   the rising   stirring   falling
falling back   into the original
I can recognize the heat   of the sun   the leaves gliding by
my smoothing face   it is all
as I assumed it would be   I have assumed it all
there is a woman walking   beside the animal
pleasant voice   syllables washing in   hair swaying
in the ease of the sun
He is there now too   running alongside
I hear his voice   lower than the others   I can say

his name too   purchase the shape of him   with my voice
Dad-e-da   a big   thirsty shape
the hum of him.
When he touches me   he gives me his weight
the certainty   of his grand voice
he appears   above me   his face dividing when   he smiles
I am sitting on   the back of the horse   the warm moving back
the tightening and slackening
in the hinges of my hips   the rhythm beating
through the pressure   of the hide
I see clearly   I see my own unliquefied   extremities
the length of my arm   ends
in a hand   the length of my leg   ends
in a foot   it is demonstrable
and for this rare   uncompromised   moment
I am secure   I cannot be deposed
I am
all the strong   unhurried length   of me
I am Stella.

Simple Animals

They are introducing me   to animals today   what they call simple animals
they turn the pages   and I watch
I long for a few hard prongs   of silence   but there is to be
no silence   only
the white scratching   of the page   and
the endless smile   unwinding
Horse.
I cannot say it   cannot pronounce   the word
but does it matter?   I see the warm   brown   girth
I remember it   I understand   but that is not enough
I must rip   out the word   and carry it to them
and because I cannot
they take my fingers   and they dig   stabbing   at the page
Horse, horse.
and they keep on swinging   at me   with their violent teeth
Horse, horse.
I hear   their voices narrowing   waiting
in horrible   alert
waiting   to drop down   upon the word
to seize   and carry it.

It is the only word   I must show   the word I cannot find
though somewhere it resides   a small stamped   shape   like a fish or a shoe
I smile   because that has calmed them   in the past
Yes, yes!   they cry
and reach their fingers out   the hand before me   reaching
like a cup   waiting again
for me   to put the word in
but I don't have   that one
and still   they turn the pages
and I wait   beneath the crouching   voices
their faces   flattened now

and I know   when I see them
that my mother   is a smooth white owl
and my father
is something like a bear.

And the Words Keep Falling

 I will not allow the sound   to pry the hinges of my skin
to open up the clear of me   and settle in
so I look up   examining her face
the center   the mouthpiece   from which
the coins and noises spill.

And the words keep falling   today they are soft   washing
against my sides like rain   I have to stiffen   to repel them
my hard and shining skin
still falling   the rain-words
and my mother is singing   it's raining   it's pouring
and her face   is above me
the eyes pouring down
but I do not think   I will let them in   today
to poison
my uncorrupted   skin
it's raining   it's pouring
he went to bed   and he bumped his head
and he couldn't get up   in the morning.

Words of Possession

It is one of the words   I know
I have only to say it   to produce
the shape   a large devotion   swaying
folding above me   a grave   delaying weight
ma-ma   it is through this word   that I enter
that I prepare   to enter
the world of startling   and grievous pressure
ma-ma
I lean against   the voice
a stack of warm   consonants
I say the word   again
and take possession.

The Smoke of My Voice

I try to protect a little space
a notion for myself   a shape of honest solitude
I describe it   with my finger   I return
the edge of the territory   they must not swallow.

They are back now
they smile   tired eyes   *Honey*
I cannot persuade them
I cannot make them understand
their steppings-in   are sacrilege
I want only the clarity   of the shape of ground
that I protect
the order of the chants   I use to clear
my little space
but they are sweeping me up   into the hurry   of their voices
I sing and my voice rises   the room is full now.

They come again   sharp-beaked
tapping away   and in the alarm
they have taken it   the smoke of my voice   has left the room.

I must
warm the room   I must
dispel the corruption   of their public sounds
I begin to sing again
they speak   in their loud   above-water voices
I sit in the corner   guarding
my precious space   waiting for their faces
to crash down
hot and brazen
their faces coming down
there is no patience long enough.

They Are So Alone

I hear their invitations   *drink with me   eat with me*
look at me   their threaded smiles
and I see   they are afraid   of solitude
I listen   to the brimming   of their language
language slopping   over everything
filling every blissful   quiet place
and I see   they are afraid   of silence.

Seeking the stickiness   of my proximity
plucking   as if they would pluck   the vivid from me
shouting together   toppling over   one another
their scrambling   empty-stomached
brightness.

Eye Contact

When I dance and sing   and try to straddle   the deviating line
they come about me
with their slicing arms
Look at me   they demand
Look at me   honey
no matter how much   I look   it is never enough
I look until
the need in their eyes
cancels me out
Look at me
their fingers   probing   ticking
at the quiet edgings   of my skin
Look at me
the smile grinding   out of them.

Hunters

They flatter me   consult the book
dive at me again
each word   I know   is tactical
each gesture   is rehearsed
trying to catch   my private sounds
with the swoop
of their butterfly-net   mouths.

The Glittering and Crying

I know where we're going   I can tell
at a glance   though she seems unsure
the fermenting trees   the stench of hot-beetled earth
the boys   their faces perpetually   open   noise streaming
from their garish   mouths
boys who run   and run   and never unwind.

We're at the park   *Stella*
the more boys there are   boys
devouring the intervals   of light
the more unlikely   the smaller   I become
as she steers me through   the glittering and crying
Let's go back to the children   *Stella*
their fingers strumming
the joined vibrations
of their bodies   *Let's go back*
again
as if I do not hear.

Dependable

I close my eyes against   the cracking of the light
they will come at me   stabbing
she holds my wrist   the path vibrates   is calmed
by my slow shadow.

Moving my weight   from foot to foot
making of myself   a pendulum
children always   in the forward motion
words charging   from their lips
there is nowhere   to be quiet.

Treading from foot to foot   shifting through
and shifting back
as my body draws
down the weight
they begin   to stagger
soon there will be   nothing left of them.

I want my face   to be quiet   all over
the same weight of clean
and unimpeded   skin
balancing   measuring
treading
to the beat   of the song   they cannot hear
striving
to make the earth
dependable.

The Experimental Air

She takes my hand   and leads me to   the swing
I used to find it necessary
pitching high   into the experimental   air
higher and higher   closer to the top   the piercing
watch the tracks   of the chains   as they joy upward   watch
the flash of my   silver self
watch   my cry extinguishing
and then   the fall begins
the flaring   piebald   insecurity   it lasts just a moment
as I pull   my body back
a pepper-shake   of weight at first
and then   the settling in
of all the dizzy parts.

Squeezing my knees together   the white chop of my feet
then up again
the fear and the cry
the surprise slipping   gravely back   as I return
then up   again
into the roaring sun.

The Swing

The chains stream upward   into the bellowing sky
how do I know it will hold me   the unreliable air?
my body becoming smaller   and steeper   and brighter
before vanishing.

Perhaps that is why they make   so much noise   the children
as they swing
at least their disappearance
will be registered.

Swimming Pool

First   I must look down   press my face against   the hardened air
feel this with my tongue   below   the conscripted figures
excavated spines
plumes sprouting   from their paddle-hands
she stands above me now   shadow fixing   the escaping air
holding the calming dark   above me   waiting
the stairs are difficult   holding for one moment   preposterously still
then dropping   reforming
surging toward   my careful bones
I must measure   the intention of each step
if I am
to travel   down
securely.

There is a man there   she always smiles at him
I smiled at him once   taking in the kindling face   the brilliant teeth
so then   I greeted him
why is it necessary   to do it again   and again
as if we have lost   our memory?

And I wait in the small room   while she dresses
I keep the indiscriminate light   at bay
dividing and apportioning   the room   with the slicing of my arm
I do not need a partner to dance   my arms un-nest the light
from every spinning source.

And it is there now   in front of me
I test the steps with my toes   pressing down against the tile
a tender increment of light   testing   torching   burning through
Stella, are you coming in?   the unnecessary words repeated
Are you coming in   to the water?
I am coming in

all the fraying parts of me   are licked together
nothing will be lost
as I press forward   it silks against my chest
but then I jump   and the cold sparks fly
splintering against my back
it dapples my face   rushes cool droplets in my eyes
I am shouting with the spring of it   and she shouts too
the open   pitching mouth   a shadow digging in
to the white water
and I am following the mouth   the stretching sound of it
I am boistering   through now   singing
and I am at the cresting point
slipping   and blazing   and returning   to creation
I am born
Five more minutes   she holds up the fingers of her hand
and I am returned   to the splitting-fence   of land
to the stairs that gobble
to the words   hidden long ago
that cannot
be returned.

Upon Arrival

A small consoling shape of skin
the back of his neck   I will look at it for hours
as we drive   the weight of the seatbelt
across my knees   the sudden appearance of my face
in the metal   larking up at me
the flowering teeth   I am buckled in
going on vacation   with them   he puts on George Harrison
and the car smells rapturously   of coconut
we are moving forward   through
the anticipation   of the music   through   the back of his neck
through   the suitcases   their persistent energetic weight
and the motion is compressed   and installed   in my new body   which
is solid now   and has just begun to hum
I can lick the music   with my tongue
the high starry notes   of the guitar.

If only we could keep   traveling like this
in expectation   the reliable pressure of the seat
the compass of warm skin   if only
we were not bound   to arrive
the opened door   dropping my body   into the sudden heat
people beating forward   sounds swooping and alighting   and   I
am afraid   when I try   to shiver through it
I will be cut   by their voices and entombed
in the great drowsy wobble-sleeves of color
the sounds are sharpening
my feet disappear   on the uncertain ground
and I try   to find myself   to pull myself
together   all the organizing bones
they are telling me to hurry   *Oh no, Stella   don't do that*
don't fall to the ground!
but I have to make sure   the ground
has not been
deleted.

And the tongues of my arms   are being squeezed
and I can tell   from their concentrated faces
and their screwdriver hands
that they do not   understand   and I will fall
into the cauldron   of the light   and the seagull cries
will scatter me
and still   they do not understand
and still
the light dismantles.

The Threshold

They meddle in beside me   the other shapes   with their chaos-mouths
the tilt of their hard breath
even a little touch
and I may topple.

This is the line   the line between
the other world   the one I had just learned to see
the world with its outside squeezing sky
the scent that falls   scent that leaves
no room for my precautions
and the pressure of these people   squirting noise
the line came down   I could not catch my foot   in time
and now   I am stranded   voices pass   collide
there is never   time
time to grow accustomed   time to make
the necessary concessions
Go on   go forward
She is there beside me   the long vertical
issuing   the usual instructions
She is there   an interrupted line
intersecting at the base
the slicing-line   the threshold.

I can hear her voice   the voice
she wields   in the turn of every crisis   anxiety kept
like a teaspoon   in her pocket
she stands   beside me with the steady voice   *It's all right, Stella*
It's all right   the voice working   until
it has gained purchase   *It's all right, Stella*
but underneath the voice   the faces beating in and out   the heat
of the collision   underneath
the shape of me   grows ragged
I close my eyes   reach out my hand

scorching through the line.
I am here now   on the other side
of the threshold
I must survive   until the next line crashes
the automatic door
parting time   separating
the hush   from
the devouring.

Swamp Song

We pass through the swamp now   I hear the insects tramping
I hear the mind of the slow-purr alligator
the alligator I see   and they do not.

The xylophone planks   of the boardwalk   the goose-flesh soil
the wires that run down   her flimsy bones
she is behind   I cannot see her   but I know
the shape of her
he turns   a dark sallow   against the darker gliding trees
there is the side of him   as he bicycles   drawing my chariot along
the bulk of him creaking   I hear the wheel
turning on the wet ground.

In between their bodies   the bicycles   the chariot
there is nothing   but the gulp
of the disappearing ground   and the wires of her bones
occasionally snapping.

She is leaning down now   *Okay, Stella, okay. Let's pull the zipper up*
and she gives me   a big costly peppermint smile
up go the teeth of the zipper   out go the teeth of
her mouth   down comes the rain.

They are both   they would have me believe   at ease
so I must sing   stretching the syllables between them   nothing
too sudden   they need order and routine
occasional punches   of flat sky   the drill of rain   vowels opening
and falling   steady and velvety and low
the line of notes   tethering me to her   and me to him   and back   through
all the wet
wet leaves to me   *We're having an adventure, Stella*
she says   and she says that because

it is raining harder   because it is pouring down
can they still hear?
she turns her face to me
I produce each note   carefully and each note falls   on the dark leaves
and is smothered.

I sing more loudly.

The labor of trying to sing   above the din
of trying to organize   the notes.
She bicycles into a tree
I'm still here!
but I know it is conditional.

It's sweet, she's singing   but it is not
sweet   it is necessary
without the music   we would be
just a little pinch of detail   a bicycle drawing a chariot   another bike
dropped into
the mud
the closing mud
the blink and the beginning.

Ocean

The bodies crunch   the voices cut
into the air around   my shoulders   shaving
the softness from my hair
someone is pulling me up   again   by the spike of my arm
Let's keep going, Stella   heard that one before   not dangerous
those words   sliding from her wrist
and now they are behind me   and the planks no longer shake
reached the edge of the boardwalk now   now I will crouch   to taste the sand
the different temperatures   of light
I drop down   my whole body folding   lovely   pliant
reach out to taste   this sand   assess
the quality   of dormant light
but   the voice traveling down   again   *No! Don't eat!*
words dropped   in front of me   rounded words   like eggs
I look up   as the egg-words roll aside   and smile   *Take off your shoes, Stella*
she is pointing at my shoes   these words   I know   and so they are precise
these shapes   stitched into the air   in front of me
Take—off—shoes   rectangle—circle—oval   I take off the shoes and
the next words drop   *Good girl, Stella*
words that turn around me
like an arm   winding
and caressing
and now she is leading me down   to the sea
across the hot sand   my toes gasp   and my ankle slides away
and now my feet are crooked   like a ginger root   and now
I watch the sea wash   in below
I am waiting   she is holding my hands   my whole body is   alert
she is behind me   she is the mark of our bodies   in the world
I am the unseen
and now it comes   the sprint of the wave   the rattling assault
strikes me   and surrounds me   pressing
against the furnishings   of skin
for a moment   I am created

where the water stops   this is the shape of me
the water has confirmed   the solid
and now the water   draws away   in a great lean rush
that tears   tears backward   so that I could not stand
without her hands   clamped across
the humming front of me
it is hurrying   there is the roar   as it shouts away
and I am left.

The whole boisterous clear
tumbles through me   and I laugh
to be made   and found!
and then it comes again   the wave
to find me
and naturally
I dance.

PART THREE

The Wizard

My daughter possessed it once
(speech)
and then she lost   it
How will it be   for us   to dwell in a wordless land?
I see a figure   a small figure wading   water   mud
the smooth before invention
in the beginning was the word   before the earth   before water   before
everything
and here I remember a man   and a woman praying
over a baby   and a bell rung   in a cold Irish castle   I must stop
running like Madeline's nun   with her hands in the air
I must be competent   and rise above   the heavy charcoal lines
I will not remember   the rampage   of my daughter's words
and their terrible   cessation
I will become   (I thought)
a woman whose emotion   whose imploring mouth
is neatly stoppered
by the artifact of truth.

I must approach   the project   with an air
of scrupulous inquiry   I will cut away   I will get   somewhere.

So I took the trouble to arm myself   with sandwiches   and a clean mind
I studied   and made a decision
I reached out to grasp   to hold it fast
and found I was dealing   with a receding   mythical   prize
I armed myself   with amulets   and magical boots
and there were people   at the side of the road   ready to sell me anything
a hundred dollars   per lovely illuminating drop
Your child has only   to swallow   a single drop   and she will speak.

And I see her silver   blooming   face
tears of light

scalding the skin   I imagine
but every night   I fall asleep
insensible
and my daughter   is no closer   to the triumph
to the act   of repossession
in my dream I am too tired   to think
I see the wizard
I see him   on the stage   leaning on a broom
dressed entirely   in black
and I know   he has brought it with him
he cannot   have forgotten
the tiny   blinking   fierce   bottle
the bottle   with the words in.

And then   coming through the night-turns   of my mind
rushing at the stage   comes the other thing   some sort of beast I cannot name
the nameless   lashing thing   but I know what it is   know it has come to take
the words away   the wizard must fight it   must push it back
and I have become the wizard
the beast comes forward   and I strike it
I hold the broom   above my head   I know
what I must do   I must
stab it through   the mouth
I have found   my enemy
this is the creature
that has been taking   words
pulling them into its coils   it is lined with them   engrossed
Kill it at the righteous point!   I strike it again and again
Now we are free!   Now she will speak!
the mouth of the beast tears   its face collapses
I have won
then I wake   and
the silence is still there   it is curling up   from the corners of the room

white   smoking   silence
I have got it wrong   all of it
my hands remember the broom   but they hold only silence.

Then I pull   myself together   (a phrase arriving from my past)   and make
another effort   I say—because I am a wizard
and I am expected   to say something
and this is   the only word I have   now—
Abracadabra.

Omens

Then I did not believe   in omens   in placing signs
where the opportunistic eye   could find them
then
before the quiet   descended
no words from the child
again no words   and again
that was before   in the slim paper yesterday
that was order
then   that was accomplishment
when each thought   naturally converted   to an action
before infinity surrounded   and preposterously
buckled
(signs can be forbidden   when the world maintains
a pleasing   voluntary   order).

Signs are everywhere   now
now   I can afford   only brief escapes   the detour of a minute
half a page   a single bird
the magic must be swallowed   quickly
so little time   to eat or sleep   or shift
through the wounds   of an ordinary day.

And so   I have come to believe
plunged   in the dangerous stillness   of the room
studying the floor   I have learned to see them
signs   coincidences
marvels.

If your child can   no longer   speak   the story goes
perhaps you will   be offered
a consolation   prize
a small simmering something
perhaps a bird.

The sight of a bird   flying
it isn't much
it is only what I make it.

So
we find symbols   and we grow them in the garage
we find a bird here   and a coin there
and we sprinkle them
on the courage   of the dark.

Clearing the Air

I watch the children
the words rise above them   papier-mâché words   striped and feathered
and as they turn   for these are social children
a coin falls   from a single pocket
and the heads fall
flawlessly
together
so this is how   such children   move.

I go on watching   the children at the party
the easy way their bodies sway   skirts lifting   braids falling
the undulating arms recalling
a shared   concealed knowledge
and the air above the children
crowding   with the buzz and crackle   of their words
oh   you're thinking   it's a metaphor
but it isn't   when you've reached a certain pitch   of desperation
metaphors   are left behind
they take too long.

Nothing is abstract anymore   my longing for speech
for the moment when words   tear
into sound
is too conspicuous.

Every day   the words take on a different form   today
a dazzle of birds   above the streaming children
tomorrow
a beetle
hurt   beneath a stone.

This is not the way it used to be   words   then
issued into the cleared air   burned free

awaiting them
my mind moved   through orderly   dedicated syllables
moved on   through the thin   flat   pacing hardness
of the words
onto the final resting   thought.

The longing changed that
roaring through   consuming
all the pinecone words
the kindling   of manageable thoughts.

My daughter spoke once   in long ecstatic sentences   and then
they were taken.

And the longing works and works
it is a solid thing   it could be scored and eaten.

I am gathering the words
I stack them   I bury them
I wait.

The Quickenings of Magic

Every day   I become more susceptible
to the quickenings   of magic.

I can still lay down   words   in the expected way—
the *click-click punch*   of staples
but that is the outside.

So now I pay attention   I look for words everywhere   because perhaps
if I pay attention   the way Scheherazade   paid attention
observing the cartography of silence....

A meeting at my daughter's school   they're discussing   the acquisition
of language   and they've handed me a questionnaire   naturally
my mind   is wandering   I wonder what
I have to do   with this
confounding enterprise   I find myself recalling
the theory—we studied it in school   when I was twelve   an example
they said   of the medieval mind
of those who came before us   the beleaguered   past ones—
the theory of spontaneous   generation   in which
a spark   might   enter a stone
startled by the fiery breath
balanced on an instant
the stone stretches   and becomes.
So easy.

What would it be like   to set your foot   on the forest floor
believing
that every ounce of earth   or moss   or leaking blue
could shiver into life?
(I've put crosses in the boxes   what do they signify?)

The leaf begins to shake

the holding air returns
and pleats the edges of the wing
(*Pragmatics?   Grammar?   Word order?*)
it's finished now   the moth   it flies away
and the sulky dampness   underneath
having been provoked
(*Verbal cue?   Level of assistance?*)
begins to slide   and tremble
 (*Accuracy level?   Forming questions?*)
everything then   could be cracked   and opened   spilling
the glorious
animating ink.

Now that I have the longing   I believe
I practice constantly
(*Expression of needs / feelings?*)
sometimes
I look at my daughter   willing the words to spring
from her lips
like diamonds
or cherry pits—
what is the fairy tale
today?

Every Frivolous Part

And what do you want?   the mother asks
as the quiet devours   the word
which was   or might have been
What do you want to take   so that   the word remains?

Take the virtue from my eyes   take the shining of my hair
take the light that used   to animate   my voice
I am giving away   every frivolous part.

I have bargained with the source   whatever name we give   the blank
that calls back favors
the older I get   the more I believe in Fate   in the sucking vacuum-chamber
of Greek
of twisted chances   and characters who meet abysmal ends
Here   with the wide-eyed fallen ones
Jocasta   Medea   Electra   you know you've fallen here   you know
you're in the dark with them   they don't teach these anymore   there is no
moral
to sew   into the leather of your shoe.

Paying for the right   to keep the word
a handful of words   gathered in the months   pressed between the sheets
of glass
preserved above
the windowsill.

The Questionnaire

The questionnaire asks   *How has having a child   with special*
needs   changed you?
do they want   the heroic answer?
The heroic   and I know how it goes
they want me   to say that I am patient now
that now   I enjoy the little   precious grooves   of life
in other words   I have learned to shovel   gratitude
into my shrinking   mouth
I have learned
to devote myself
to the private   recital of blessing
I have become
an exemplary citizen.

Yes   it has changed me
I watch other children pass   I eye them in their glittering   ease
their inattentive
good fortune.

I watch them
the scavenging bird   who looks   but cannot steal
stealing a glance
most of all   it has changed   my body
doubt   has sewn the seams   along my skin   doubt
has settled in   so that now   I cannot be lifted
and then there is patience   spreading
and under that   the raging   I read
about these happy   dazzling   mother-creatures
and today   I think
I will take their bodies   and render them   down
for fat
it is a moment   for grim   old   fairy tales   and truth

for cauldrons   and revenge
but what they want
is the Joan-of-Arc-Madonna
the warrior   whose wounds   bleed milk.

Conversations

There is so much   in these conversations   we cannot say
the conversations   between the stifled   mothers and of course
that is not   a convenient word   occasionally
people talk   of despair   (that's okay)   And how
are you today?
Well   I think   something resembling
a charred   and   winged creature
swooping down   with the demented eye.

Not so bad   thank you   is the permitted answer   so I refrain
Oh   I'm Good   she says
and she has chosen   to refrain   she has obeyed
and we are broken   quite broken   and yet
we are still   in charge   of the important things
our bodies   are still clean   our hair is kempt   we have obeyed again
sometimes   I crave the freedom   to be stricken
to simply   wail
I would be   Rumpelstiltskin
jumping   until I break
in two
And how are *you*
today?

Positively Quiet

The book tells me to be positive   I hold the book at arm's length
Positive   I think of the word   as something one   ingests
like a reverse   suicide pill
if only I could swallow it   something to permeate   and convert
my sour flesh
if only I could swallow it   like faith
Be Positive   perhaps   I think   it is a sort of unguent   something
to seal my skin   against
the dangerous   and   zealous air
committing my body   to receive
transmissions   of happy unreality
to cut off the air   to cut off all access   to the air   so that
as I gradually   expire
sweetly   contentedly   in an orderly manner
I will know   this is the way
I am supposed to go
Positively
quiet.

The Park

She runs across the grass   in small   bright   kicks   She is so quick
the grass blurs   She jumps onto the seat   polishing   She
grabs the chains   She does everything   without hesitation
Her mouth immediately open   Her intentions immediately
converted   into words
it happens   so quickly   it seems
immodest
but of course   She is one of those   I think
body cut out   with pinking shears
buzzing   in the heat
Her wishes   so obvious   She glistens with them
there are so many of Her.

Even now as I watch   She is gesturing   calling
it happens so fast.

I am waiting   for the possibility   of an indication
it is all about   waiting
I try not to notice   this noise   this extraordinary quickness
this shattering   dexterity
I am gradually   absorbing   the possibilities
of what could happen   if I wait.

She has spoken   to Her mother   (now   the girl)
She has protested   word-spitting   all in a few   seconds
such virtuosity   is fierce.

Patience   they used to tell me   is a virtue
so says the teacher   to the child   so says
the man to the little   whale-boned   woman
so   they always say   those who have   the power
those who never   have to wait   and as I wait
and wait   my face changes
soon it will be leveled.

Mother Goose

The mother turns   before my eyes
into a goose   sleek and white   and wobbling with   good fortune
stuffed with it   down her thick throat   the goose will be amazed I think
to hear that her daughter   has spoken
but the goose carries   smoothly on
there is nothing   but a small accustomed   smile
so then   I remind myself   she is one of those   who do not   know
the world is divided now   into those who know
and those who don't
and everything
that seemed to matter   before
has been forgotten.

I'm trying to recall   the names
of the hoods   they used once   to extinguish
the flames   of candles
and give me the names
of a few other   obsolete   household items
the spindle   the mangle   the blotter
how many houses   for example
now possess
just the right   sort of   bone
a traveling bone
to lodge   in the throat
a bone   for the goose
in her splendid   maturity
to swallow.

A Few Pathetic Thoughts on Jealousy

As I go about   the ministrations of the day   climbing
from one appointment   to the next   glancing
at my watch   and winding up discretion
attempting to suppress   the more godforsaken thoughts
I watch myself   as I begin   to change
the large affrighted eyes   the baggy flesh
again today   I read of an acquaintance   someone I used to know   someone
I walked beside   in equal
expectation   I read
of their achievements   stacked
on the monumental shelf
awards and books   and recognition
the prince is in front   of me
and I've become   the toad
freckled skin   and quiet breathing
the crouch   that lends itself   to waiting
in the corner of the room.

The Original Mud

Here I sit on the edge
the concrete around the pond   has just hardened
all my effort is bent   on remaining solid
I wear a blue suit   slit up the middle by a silver zipper   on my lap I hold
a bowl of gooseberries   my head bent   my tongue between my lips   I taste
the sour water-flesh   I am my daughter's age   my face is her face
it startles   me
the anticipation   of her smile
secretive and narrow   the grooves   of the down-turned eyes   the hair
that was mine
and is not mine now   heavy   fur-belly brown
the water behind me has not yet become a pond   it's just water   empty clear
the girl on the edge   has not yet become
she is striving   to remain   to keep the lines separate
the lines of the face   lines of the eyes   and the mouth
don't let them soften   don't let them drown
the hair of the girl in the picture   cannot be my hair   the hair of a
sharp young animal   before nature starts   to take away
if I cannot hold my smile up
if I cannot settle my legs into   their assigned positions
if I cannot find the letters   and fix them   if I cannot knock the sense
of it all   into my dyslexic skull
the sense of the letters   the sense of
detonating words   I will not appear   I will fall
swallowing the word-water   syllables lapping in the original dark.

It is all to come   in the picture
now   as I contemplate the fruit   sliding my tongue   now I am simply greed
now I am   the surprise of   skin
and the pleasure of being   alone
but I will grow
into a new head of hair   a shine of new words

my daughter will be born
she sits on the edge   again   and will she fall?
will she keep the lines straight?   the lines she must learn   the lines
she must hold
or will she be   dispatched
into the freedom of the dark?

The Gooseberry Picture Again

In this picture   the idea of regret   is still abstract
the idea of history   unpossessed
it's hard to believe   looking at the picture   that we were ever thus
whole and simple and unentailed
in this picture I am two years old   I am simply greed
with my basin of fruit
the covetous anticipation   of my tongue
but one thing will not change
it is always about the language   of possession
Are we in?   Are we out?   invited
or excluded?
the words change
but the appetite does not.

On Being Still

Stella is sitting in her chair   for a child
she is expertly still
the silence pressing   out
the quiver of a hum   inside the mouth
she holds a block   between her hands   only the fingers move
spinning   it is not just a spinning motion   one of the words   one of the
words
we take out   of the cereal box   each morning   it is also
the obsolete ancestral motion   drawing out the thread
I pick up a block   crouch beside her
trying to be quiet   I stream the fixity of my eyes across   her face
I set the block   in motion   *quick quick shuffle*
my fingers are immense
I am trying to notch   the thoughts in place   *quick quick shuffle*
there are those   who would call her expression
absent   but that is only
if we make ourselves   the starting point.

The stillness
I find myself observing others   the order of their muscles   in repose
what makes their faces   different?
most of us keep   our spirits flickering   waiting
to convert   to reassign our tension
at the slightest indication
from another
faces brushing when they do not touch.

Stella does not reflect   the whims   of others
all moves originate with her.

I smile   hoping that my smile   will find an answer in her face   moving
my smile over her face   as the moon moves   over water
forgetting   of course   what I have just learned.

Her fingers spin   a humming-grind   escaping
from her closed mouth   I move away
when she and I   occupy a room
I must calculate the value   and strategies   of space
I calculate distances   all the time   now
she falls against me   humming   in a cloud of yellow light
she grips me   mouth stretched   so I see the teeth
bestowing her lips   on my hair
the eyes
have found me
sometimes   she nudges me   from the corner of her eye
sharp   complicit   sometimes
I am hoisted   spitted   on the pupil
and sometimes   I am not seen.

I used to attempt   to be   moderate in my expression   to cultivate
a skeptical soul
but here   it is that world   the world of moderation
that seems delusional   and quaint   here
we pass from days   of dark-age grim   equipped   with the gnashing of teeth
to days of awe   days when I watch   her body   in the water
when I watch   the water fall   in peals   over her laughing head
I cannot remember   the last time
we passed
a sensible day.

A Single Gulp

My dreams have begun   to take on   a simplicity   that is crushing
they present themselves   in single gulps
last night I came upon myself   I could not move
I had been painted   blue
my legs were fused   my body made of tin
I tried to move   to break through   the senseless skin
I encountered something hard
a strange   exclusionary element
Well   said the voice   *you've come up against it*
You've come up against
the element   of surprise
You've been
seized by it.

And since I am a top
I spin
spinning   laughing
seized.

Music, or Evidence of Stella

The favorite today is *Sly   and the Family   Stone*
I turn the volume up   she is laughing   she comes toward me   comes
to take in   the music
this is what I cannot explain
to the clinicians   they see
the absences
the words wound back   into the spool (and I see too   under the puncturing
eye)
but they do not see
Stella dancing   to *Sly and the Family Stone*.

Watching her   I realize   that I have never listened
music has never   startled my skin
this is what they mean   by ecstasy   this is what they mean
by living.

I have gone back   through the photos of my family
their calm faces   reserved
for the enamel   on salt and pepper shakers
I look at the careful faces   held
still   in preparation
for the approved reproduction
faces that are proud
of not betraying
surprise
and I cannot find any evidence
of Stella.

Hope

Without hope   they say
you couldn't go on
but we do   in almost every house
we rise   in the morning   we brush our hair
and inspect   the embers
of the face.

I used to wonder   with the malevolent accuracy
of the average child
why we couldn't all   go naked
the pleading root   of the body
hungry   and ineligible   (we might have glimpsed it
in the morning   if we had time   which we didn't because
we were busy
gripping the button   pulling it through)
by the time we had completed
all the little ceremonies
of dressing
we had
forgotten
what it was
we didn't want to see
(if you catch it   for a moment
keep on cranking   winding up the costume   whatever form
the allowance   takes   today).

By the time   we've brushed our hair   and made the coffee
put on deodorant   (and some of us pray)
we've quite   forgotten
the terror
galloping
in the tenderness
of each soft hand.

ACKNOWLEDGMENTS

Thank you to:

Rebecca Kaiser Gibson for selecting my manuscript, for hearing my voice.
To everyone at Bauhan publishing for their kindness, generosity and care.

To Victor, for your constancy and love through all times, joyful and hard,
wonderful and soul-defying.
To Stella. You are always in my heart, my beautiful, extraordinary daughter.
Keep embarking to see bliss (you know what I mean).
To Carol Stewart, for your wholehearted friendship and support. I can't say
how much they mean to me.
To Siri France, across all the years we've known each other. For your friend-
ship and encouragement. For saying, 'keep writing, keep trying.'
To Elizabeth Burns, for your deep and honest friendship. I am so glad I sent
you an email out of the blue. Your novel was a light to me when I needed one.
To the creek beside which I am allowed to walk.
To birds, for existing.
For every moment in nature.

Thanks to the following magazines in which some of these poems first ap-
peared:

Cincinnati Review: "Horse"
Mid-American Review: "The Walls Will Be Silenced When She Speaks"
Natural Bridge: "Hope"
Prairie Schooner: "The Waiting Room"
Slippery Elm: "Where Does the Fury Come From?"

The May Sarton New Hampshire Poetry Prize

The May Sarton New Hampshire Poetry Prize is named for May Sarton, the renowned novelist, memoirist, poet, and feminist (1912–1995) who lived for many years in Nelson, New Hampshire, not far from Peterborough, home of William L. Bauhan Publishing. In 1967, she approached Bauhan and asked him to publish her book of poetry, *As Does New Hampshire*. She wrote the collection to celebrate the bicentennial of Nelson, and dedicated it to the residents of the town.

May Sarton was a prolific writer of poetry, novels, and perhaps what she is best known for—nonfiction on growing older (*Recovering: A Journal, Journal of Solitude*, among others). She considered herself a poet first, though, and in honor of that and to celebrate the centenary of her birth in 2012, Sarah Bauhan, who inherited her father's small publishing company, launched the prize. (www.bauhanpublishing.com/may-sarton-prize)

PAST MAY SARTON WINNERS:

In *The Wreck of Birds*, the first winner of Bauhan Publishing's May Sarton New Hampshire Poetry Prize, Rebecca Givens Rolland embraces an assimilation of internal feeling and thought with circumstances of the natural world and the conflicts and triumphs of our human endeavors. Here, we discover a language that seeks to at once replicate and transcend experiences of loss and disaster, and together with the poet "we hope that such bold fates will not forget us." Even at the speaker's most vulnerable moments, when "Each word we'd spoken / scowls back, mirrored in barrels of wind" these personal poems insist on renewal. With daring honesty and formal skill, *The Wreck of Birds* achieves a revelatory otherness—what Keats called the "soul-making task" of poetry.

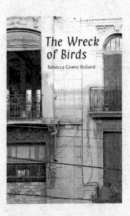

—**WALTER E. BUTTS**, New Hampshire Poet Laureate (2009–2013), and author of *Cathedral of Nervous Horses: New and Selected Poems*, and *Sunday Evening at the Stardust Café*

The poetry of Rebecca Givens Rolland has previously appeared in journals including *Colorado Review, American Letters & Commentary, Denver Quarterly, Witness*, and the *Cincinnati Review*, and she is the recipient of the Andrew W. Mellon Fellowship, the Clapp Fellowship from Yale University, an Academy of American Poets Prize, and the Dana Award.

Nils Michals won the second May Sarton New Hampshire Poetry Prize in 2012, and has also written the book *Lure*, which won the Lena-Miles Wever Todd award in 2004. His poetry has been featured in *The Bacon Review, diode, White Whale Review, Bay Poetics, The Laurel Review* and *Sonora Review*. Most recently he published *Gem Box* (The Word Worls, 2019). He lives in Santa Cruz, California and teaches at West Valley College.

Nils Michals is alternately healed and wounded by the tension between the timeless machinations of humankind and the modern machinery that lifts us beyond—and plunges us back to—our all-too-human, earthly selves. Supported by minimally narrative, page-oriented forms, his poems transcribe poetry's intangibles—love, loss, hope, a sense of the holy—in a language located somewhere between devotional and raw, but they mourn and celebrate as much of what is surreal in today's news as of what is familiar in the universal mysteries . . . *Come Down to Earth* is a 'long villa with every door thrown open'"

—**ALICE B. FOGEL**, New Hampshire Poet Laureate (2014–2019),
and author of *A Doubtful House* Bauhan Publishing, 2017)

David Koehn won the third May Sarton New Hampshire Poetry Prize in 2013. His poetry and translations were previously collected in two chapbooks, *Tunic*, (speCt! books 2013) a small collection of some of his translations of *Catullus*, and *Coil* (University of Alaska, 1998), winner of the Midnight Sun Chapbook Contest. He lives with his family in Pleasanton, California.

David Koehn's first book, *Twine*, never falters—one strong poem after another. This is the work of a mature poet. His use of detail is not only precise and evocative; it's transformative."
—**JEFF FRIEDMAN**, 2013 May Sarton New Hampshire Poetry Prize judge and author of *Pretenders*

David Koehn's imagination, rambunctious and abundant, keeps its footing: a sense of balance like his description of fishing: "Feeling the weight . . . of the measurement of air." That sense of weight and air, rhythm and fact, the ethereal and the brutal, animates images like boxers of the bare-fist era: "Hippo-bellied/And bitter, bulbous in their bestiary masks." An original and distinctively musical poet.
—**ROBERT PINSKY**, United States Poet Laureate, 1997-2000 and author of *Selected Poems*, among numerous other collections

Deborah Gorlin won the 2014 May Sarton New Hampshire Poetry Prize. She has published in *Poetry*, *Antioch Review*, *American Poetry Review*, *Seneca Review*, *The Massachusetts Review*, *The Harvard Review*, *Green Mountains Review*, *Bomb*, *Connecticut Review*, *Women's Review of Books*, *New England Review*, and *Best Spiritual Writing 2000*. Gorlin also won the 1996 White Pine Poetry Press Prize for her first book of poems, *Bodily Course*. She holds an MFA from the University of California/Irvine. Since 1991, she has taught writing at Hampshire College, where she serves as co-director of the Writing Program. She is currently a poetry editor at *The Massachusetts Review*.

In poem after poem in *Life of the Garment*, Deborah Gorlin clothes us in her fabric of sung words, with characters unique and familiar, and facsimiles of love that open and close their eyes, comfort, and gaze upon us. Read this fine collection—you will see for yourself.

—**GARY MARGOLIS**, 2014 May Sarton New Hampshire Poetry Prize judge and author of *Raking the Winter Leaves*. and *Museum of Islands*

Desirée Alvarez won the 2015 May Sarton New Hampshire Poetry Prize. She is a poet and painter who has received numerous awards for her written and visual work, including the Glenna Luschei Award from *Prairie Schooner*, the Robert D. Richardson Non-Fiction Award from *Denver Quarterly*, and the Willard L. Metcalf Award from the American Academy of Arts and Letters. She has published in *Poetry*, *Boston Review*, and *The Iowa Review*, and received fellowships from Yaddo, Poets House, and New York Foundation for the Arts. Alvarez received her MFA from School of Visual Arts and BA from Wesleyan University. Testing the

boundaries of image and language through interdisciplinary work, as a visual poet she exhibits widely and teaches at CUNY, The Juilliard School, and Artists Space.

These poems often shot shivers up my spine. Some made me cry. This is a book I'll want to read over and over.

—**MEKEEL MCBRIDE**, 2015 May Sarton New Hampshire Poetry Prize judge and author of
Dog Star Delicatessen: New and Selected Poems

Zeina Hashem Beck won the 2016 May Sarton New Hampshire Poetry Prize. *Louder than Hearts* melds English and Arabic, focusing on language throughout.

Beck is a Lebanese poet. Her first collection, *To Live in Autumn*, won the 2013 Backwaters Prize; her chapbook, *3arabi Song* (2016), won the 2016 Rattle Chapbook Prize, and her chapbook, *There Was and How Much There Was* (2016), was a smith|doorstop Laureate's Choice, selected by Carol Ann Duffy. Her work has won Best of the Net, been nominated for the Pushcart Prize, the Forward Prize, and appeared in *Ploughshares*, *Poetry*, and *The Rialto*, among others. Beck's most recent book is *O*, published by Penguin Random House. She lives in California

"I don't know how Zeina Hashem Beck is able to do this. Her poems feel like whole worlds. Potent conversations with the self, the soul, the many landscapes of being, and the news that confounds us all—her poems weave two languages into a perfect fabric of presence, with an almost mystical sense of pacing and power."

—**NAOMI SHIHAB NYE**

Jen Town won the 2017 May Sarton New Hampshire Poetry Prize. *The Light of What Comes After* is an autobiographical mosaic of memory and dreams that speaks to all of us trying to make some semblance of aging and what it means to live well. Jen Town's poetry has appeared in *Mid-American Review, Cimarron Review, Epoch, Third Coast, Lake Effect, Crab Orchard Review, Unsplendid, Bellingham Review,* and others. Born in Dunkirk, New York and growing up in Erie, Pennsylvania, Town went on to earn her MFA in Creative Writing from The Ohio State University in 2008. She lives in Columbus, Ohio, with her wife, Carrie.

"*The Light of What Comes After* offers a sure manifesto against the domestic and cosmetic. Town's rich linguistic moments and surprising imagery lend her voice a slant which can seem playful and unafraid, but warning is always stitched just below the surface. This is a writer who knows 'Your debts / are more than you'll ever pay back.'"

—**JENNIFER MILITELLO**, 2017 May Sarton New Hampshire Poetry Prize judge and author of *A Camouflage of Specimens and Garments*

Marilee Richards won the 2018 May Sarton New Hampshire Poetry Prize. Richards learned poetry from Charles Entrekin and others after she wandered into a workshop put on by the Berkeley, CA, Poet's Co-op in the eighties while working as an adoption interviewer for Alameda County. Richards attended the workshops for several years prior to the organization dissolving and her move to Arizona in 2001. Her poems have been published in many journals, including *The Yale Review, The Southern Review, Rattle, Poetry Northwest, The Journal,* and *The Sun.* She is the author of *A Common Ancestor* (Hip Pocket Press, 2000), and in 2016 she won the William Matthews Poetry Prize.

This is a poet with range—sympathies, anger, tragedy, other people, love, humor. . . . Richards writes unsentimental poems that road-trip through our times and look around at who is with us when we stop to fill up our cars at gas stations, [who] has been with us in offices . . . she reminds us of what the country has gained in consciousness and freedom, . . . what sorrows and suicides we have left necessarily behind, as the bus pulls up at the curb in the don't-you-get-it-yet years we have been motoring through lately.

—**DAVID BLAIR**, judge of the 2018 May Sarton New Hampshire Poetry Prize, and author of *Friends with Dogs* and *Arsonville*

Dorsey Craft is a PhD candidate in poetry at Florida State University. In addition to winning the May Sarton New Hampshire Poetry Prize, she has published her first chapbook, *The Pirate Anne Bonny Dances the Tarantella*, (Cutbank, 2020). Her work has appeared in *Colorado Review, Crab Orchard Review, Greensboro Review, Massachusetts Review, Ninth Letter, Passages North, Poetry Daily, Southern Indiana Review, Thrush Poetry Journal* and elsewhere. She holds an MFA in poetry from McNeese State University and is the Poetry Editor for *The Southeast Review*.

You will love Dorsey Craft's rollicking persona, pirate Anne Bonny, who serves up heaps of scintillant treasures from the bottomless trunk of her imagination, wit, and verve. In *Plunder*, Jack Sparrow has met his match.

—**DEB GORLIN**, judge, 2019 May Sarton New Hampshire Poetry Prize, and author of *Life of the Garment*.

In *Plunder* Dorsey Craft creates a ripple in the time-space continuum and brings 17th century pirate Anne Bonny to the 21st century. In these intense and erotic poems Bonny's wild and passionate life finds a place in the heart and mind of a contemporary woman and her struggle for love and freedom. This is a luminous and lyric debut.

—**BARBARA HAMBY**, author of *Bird Odyssey*

ALEXA DORAN is the 2020 winner of the May Sarton New Hampshire Poetry Prize and is the author of the chapbook, *Nightsink, Faucet Me a Lullaby* (Bottlecap Press 2019). She is currently a PhD candidate at Florida State University.

Her series of poems about the women of Dada, "The Octopus Breath on Her Neck," was recently released as part of Oxidant/Engine's BoxSet Series Vol 2.

You can also look for work from Doran in recent or issues of *Los Angeles Review, Mud Season Review, Salamander, Pithead Chapel* and *New Delta Review*, among others. She lives with her son in Tallahassee, Florida

Alexa Doran's *DM Me, Mother Darling* begins with a quote from J. M. Barrie's *Peter Pan*, in which little Michael asks his mother, "Can anything harm us?" Throughout the book, Mother Darling, who has lost her children, and the mother of a young boy, who tries to prepare her son for the world, speak to this seemingly ordinary question. However, as titles such as "Mother Darling Smokes a Spliff" and "For My Son, Who Asks Me to Replay Lizzo's 'Juice'" suggest, Doran casts these two women in wildly imaginative and compelling scenarios. The result is a book full of wit and wisdom. I can't recall the last time that a debut poetry collection made me laugh so hard or filled me with such surprise and wonder.

—**BLAS FALCONER**, author of *Forgive the Body This Failure*

RICHARD SMITH is the 2021 winner of the May Sarton New Hampshire Poetry Prize and this is his first book of poetry. He began life as an English major. After graduating from Princeton, he worked in publishing for twelve years. In his thirties, he retooled as a clinical psychologist, earning his Ph.D. from the University of Maryland, College Park, and he now maintains a private practice in Washington, D.C.

He and his partner live with their two dogs, who inspired the sonnet-writing that led to this book.

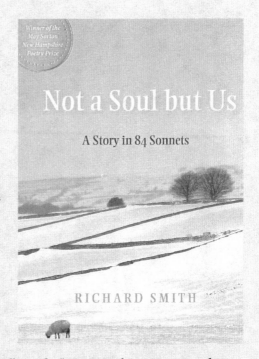

Winner of the May Sarton New Hampshire Poetry Prize

Not a Soul but Us

A Story in 84 Sonnets

RICHARD SMITH

Judge Meg Kearney says of Richard's work: "*Not a Soul But Us* is an achievement on every front. Set in rural England during and after the bubonic plague pandemic of 1348–49, this verse novel drives to the heart of what we humans are capable of when boiled down to our very core in the struggle to survive—and how, in more ways than one, it's not our intelligence or our resiliency but love and the non-human animals that save us. Timely, remarkable, and unforgettable, these eighty-four sonnets are so well crafted that we cease to notice the form, swept away as we are by the current of the story and its song."

Not since A. E. Housman's 1896 *The Shropshire Lad* has a poet produced such an endearing classic as *Not a Soul but Us* . . . Told in spare, authentic language reflecting the Anglo-Saxon world of Medieval Yorkshire, the sequence describes an orphaned boy and his dog who bond to survive, along with their sheep, during and after the bubonic plague. Each sonnet flows into the next with a natural cadence; readers will pause on the masterful couplets.

—**PAULA DEITZ**, editor of *The Hudson Review*